SONG of SOLOMON

God's best for love, marriage, sex and romance

All Scripture quotations are taken from
the New American Standard Version
unless otherwise noted.

1st Edition published 1995
2nd Edition published 1999
3rd Edition published 2005
4th Edition published 2007
5th Edition published 2011

ISBN 1-928828-12-4
ISBN 978-1-928828-12-9

Published
by

THE HUB

3405 Milton Avenue, Suite 207
Dallas, TX 75205

www.gotothehub.com

Printed in the United States of America

ECCLESIASTES A Life Well Lived (A Study of Ecclesiastes)
Bible Study Series by Tommy Nelson
4 DVD Curriculum
Companion Study Guide
A Life Well Lived paperback book

LOVELIFE Song of Solomon
Bible Study Series by Mark Driscoll
4 DVD Curriculum
Companion Study Guide
Packages and bulk discounts available

PHILIPPIANS To Live is Christ & to Die is Gain
Bible Study Series by Matt Chandler
4 DVD Curriculum
Companion Study Guide
Packages and bulk discounts available

ROMANS The Letter that Changed the World, Vol. I & II
Bible Study Series by Tommy Nelson
DVD Curriculum
Companion Study Guide
Packages and bulk discounts available

RUTH Your God. My God. A True Story of Love & Redemption
Bible Study Series by Tommy Nelson
DVD Curriculum
Companion Study Guide
Packages and bulk discounts available

SONG OF SOLOMON Enhanced for Students
DVD Curriculum byTommy Nelson
Re-mastered Video & Audio
All new graphics & menus
Never before seen Q&A's
All in one study guide for both students & leaders

VINTAGE JESUS Timeless Answers to Timely Questions
Bible Study Series by Mark Driscoll
4 DVD Curriculum
Companion Study Guide
Packages and bulk discounts available

acknowledgements

The Hub would like to thank the following friends, without whose help, this series and study guide would not have been possible:

Tommy Nelson
Robert Emmitt, Paul Staffel, Carl Huffaker, Diane Beavers and
  Community Bible Church, San Antonio, TX
John Lindell, Brad Wicks, Terry Weaver and James River Assembly,
  Springfield, MO
Brian Goins
Shatrine Krake, Krake Designs
David and Luke Edmonson and Edmonson Studios
John Dempsey and Providence Media Group
Sandra Orellana
PocketPak Albums

about the hub

Thanks for taking a moment to learn more about us. Our organization began in 1995 working with one speaker, Tommy Nelson and one amazing message, The Song of Solomon. It was and is our privilege to help champion God's written Word on Love, Dating, Marriage and Sex based directly on Song of Solomon. It is a book that has been censored for centuries and it has been a total blessing and thrill to see it change my life, and millions of others.

As of August 2009 we have rebranded our organization to reflect the root of our passion and the future of our organization:

To Develop, Find and Share life changing Bible Centric tools that move people forward. We have renamed our organization to The Hub. It is our passion and commitment to be a Hub for unique, challenging and grace filled resources. I hope you will agree after you participate and interact with one of our resources.

God Bless you and know that if you will listen, God's Truth will move you forward in life, no matter where you have been or are currently.

Doug Hudson, *President - The Hub*

The **Song of Solomon** has always been one of the mystery books of the Bible. Written in poetic style and full of Hebrew metaphors and analogies, few have ever written or spoken about it as a real story of love and relationship between Solomon and Shulammite.

But in the early 1990's, Tommy Nelson, the Pastor of Denton Bible Church in Denton, Texas, decided to teach through the book for his congregation. Then in 1994, Tommy taught the **Song of Solomon** to METRO Bible Study – a popular singles Bible study at Prestonwood Baptist Church in Plano, Texas. It was wildly popular, growing the study from 800 to 4000+ in just a few weeks. The truths found in Song of Solomon had obviously struck a chord with people and were changing lives in the process.

Based on this, the original **Song of Solomon** series was recorded in 1995 and the **Song of Solomon** Conference was launched a couple of years later. The popularity of this message was furthered as radio programs like Focus on the Family and FamilyLife aired the series and more people were exposed to it.

The **Song of Solomon** curriculum has spread throughout the world and is considered the premiere series on God's design for relationships. It was revised and updated in 2005. Since 1998, the live **Song of Solomon** Conference has been hosted at many of the leading churches across America and has reached over 100,000 people. After eight years of teaching at live conferences, Tommy Nelson, our speaker emeritus, has passed the baton on to several new speakers to continue the work he started of exposing the truths of this long-neglected book to a world that is seeking real truth from God on His design for relationships.

We trust that you will see how God's truth on relationships, as recorded in scripture by Solomon, will change your life forever.

using this study guide:
for personal study or in a small group setting

This study guide is perfect for individuals or couples who are looking for ways to deepen their relationship and find practical ways to apply the timeless truths of Scripture to their love life. It is also a great tool to use with small groups, Bible Studies and Sunday school classes.

The curriculum is designed as either a six week or eleven week study. Each of the eleven video sessions is approximately 25 minutes long and follows a simple pattern: watch/listen to a session and then discuss the questions in the study guide.

The teacher in the curriculum, Tommy Nelson, introduces and closes each session. You won't want to miss out on his exhortations!

Each chapter in the guide ends with a weekly challenge and an opportunity to pray for those in your group.

If you are a small group leader, thanks for having the courage to shepherd others along the way.

There is not a separate leader's guide. Leaders are truly facilitators of the material: there are no specific right or wrong answers to the questions. These questions are designed to spur discussion and interaction based on the truths found in Song of Solomon.

before each session
we would encourage leaders to:

- *Pray* - *Ask the Lord for guidance on how to lead the sheep in your care. Pray that He will show you ways to stimulate genuine, dynamic, and open communication.*

- *Preview* - *It is very beneficial to watch the session before you facilitate it. You will notice the key points that come to the surface and you can generate follow-up questions.*

- *Prepare* - *A small group will only go as deep and be as transparent as the leader. If a leader or facilitator is not willing to get personal, then the group will float on the surface. Let God speak through your own struggles and weaknesses.*

For Those Leading Singles/College Students: While sessions 1-4 deal with attraction, dating and courtship, you will notice that sessions 5-11 move heavily into marriage related topics. This is a great opportunity to focus the group on how to prepare for a satisfying marriage by learning these truths now. As Tommy Nelson likes to say, "It's more preventive counseling than instruction for the moment." Regardless of the relationship(s) modeled while growing up, everyone can learn better and more Biblical ways to prepare for a successful marriage.

For Those Leading Married Couples: You might think the first four sessions dealing with "before marriage" may not apply to married couples. However, the Biblical principles of attraction, dating, and courtship can bring vitality to a marriage many years after the wedding. Always be looking to see how the Holy Spirit can help you apply every passage of Scripture to the lives and relationships of married couples.

Also, there is one brief note on the production of the audio and video versions of this curriculum. This study was taped at a conference before a live audience. Tommy Nelson presented this series in six sessions. Therefore, occasionally you may notice a few "hard cuts" where the sessions were divided into two segments. Our apologies if it is any way distracting.

Attraction

Solomon wrote over 1000 songs
(1 Kgs. 4:32) as well as a
number of Psalms..
Two of his Psalms dealt with
weddings (Ps.

He is physically delightful ——————

His character is pure or holy ————

He was popular ————

She considers herself privileged ———
to be his wife..

.. in the intimacy of his home ————

The "daughters of Jerusalem".
A kind of chorus that asks key
questions that develop the
narrative. They declare Solomon worthy

After the man's character is ————
highlighted, now the woman's

She too is physically attractive but
character surpasses looks

1.
She is hardworking.. a servant

2.   i.e. her brothers ————
She is obedient to authority ————

her physical appearance

1 The Song of Songs, which is Solomon's.

2 "May he kiss me with the kisses of his mouth!

For your love is better than wine."

3 "Your oils have a pleasing fragrance,

Your name is like purified oil;

Therefore the maidens love you."

4 "Draw me after you and let us run together!

The king has brought me into his chambers.

We will rejoice in you and be glad;

We will extol your love more than wine.

Rightly do they love you."

5 "I am black but lovely,

O daughters of Jerusalem,

Like the tents of Kedar,

Like the curtains of Solomon."

6 "Do not stare at me because I am swarthy,

For the sun has burned me.

My mother's sons were angry with me;

They made me caretaker of the vineyards,

But I have not taken care of my own vineyard."

7"Tell me, O you whom my soul loves,
Where do you pasture your flock,
Where do you make it lie down at noon?
For why should I be like one who veils herself
Beside the flocks of your companions?"

8 "If you yourself do not know,
Most beautiful among women,
Go forth on the trail of the flock
And pasture your young goats
By the tents of the shepherds."

3 She is morally upright.
Committed to purity.

the prostitutes (Gen. 38:15)
who veiled themselves.
She will meet a man in the light not in
the darkness of sin

She is encouraged to seek such a man by
the daughters of Jerusalem

Where do you turn for answers to your deepest relationship questions?

questions like:

What should I look for in a mate?

Why and how should I date?

How do I know when I am ready to marry?

What are the keys to a great marriage?

What is the secret to a fulfilling sex life in marriage?

How do I handle conflict when it comes up in my relationship?

How can I insure that my marriage will not just survive, but thrive?

You won't find these answers on the grocery store magazine racks or in internet chat rooms. You won't find them on daytime television, prime time cable, or at your local movie theater. Try your bookshelf... or maybe even your coffee table. The secrets to great romance, marriage, and sex *are no secrets* - they were written three thousand years ago in the Bible. If you are like most people, you've probably read parts of the Scripture but have skipped over those pages known as the **Song of Solomon**.

What a book to miss! It has the distinction of being the only book to be edited and censured by the Christian church. For centuries young Jewish boys were not even permitted to read these eight chapters. Many modern readers skip over these pages, even fewer understand what's written in them, and hardly anyone will touch it on Sunday morning. Yet it is the one book that God uses to guide, direct, and teach us, as men and women, about our deepest longings. While tabloids and talk shows tempt us with empty promises, through timeless principles, the Author of marriage, sex and romance guarantees us real intimacy and promises to guide us through the perilous paths of dating on to a lifelong, fulfilling marriage.

So join with us now as we learn God's design for relationships.

1

session one | the art of attraction

Song of Solomon 1:1-8

May he kiss me with the kisses of his mouth!
For your love is better than wine.

*W*hat's attractive?

Fetching eyes? Buff biceps? A svelte figure?

God made our hearts to skip a beat and palms to sweat when we are physically attracted to someone. But judging by magazines at the grocery store checkouts, one would think an air-brushed complexion and buns of steel are the only qualifiers to loveliness. Such beauty is impossible to attain, focuses solely on external characteristics, and greatly diminishes over time.

In 1513, Ponce de Leon landed in Florida searching for the legendary fountain of youth. What evaded him then, still evades us today. We may not look to mystical water, but we believe in a magical scalpel. Our culture engages in a battle to stop the aging process because we truly believe beauty is only skin deep.

It's fitting that the first section in our study on relationships starts with attraction. The same man who wrote this book said in Proverbs, "Charm is deceitful and beauty is vain, but a woman who fears the Lord will be praised." Another way to translate the word vain is brief.

Beauty that's only skin deep won't produce deep love. Whether looking for a spouse or loving a spouse, we will learn that what's attractive in God's mind increases over time, focuses on internal characteristics, and can be attained by anyone.

1 The Song of Songs, which is Solomon's.

2 "May he kiss me with the kisses of his mouth!
For your love is better than wine."

3 "Your oils have a pleasing fragrance,
Your name is like purified oil;
Therefore the maidens love you."

4 "Draw me after you and let us run together!
The king has brought me into his chambers.
We will rejoice in you and be glad;
We will extol your love more than wine.
Rightly do they love you."

5 "I am black but lovely,
O daughters of Jerusalem,
Like the tents of Kedar,
Like the curtains of Solomon."

6 "Do not stare at me because I am swarthy,
For the sun has burned me.
My mother's sons were angry with me;
They made me caretaker of the vineyards,
But I have not taken care of my own vineyard."

7 "Tell me, O you whom my soul loves,
Where do you pasture your flock,
Where do you make it lie down at noon?
For why should I be like one who veils herself
Beside the flocks of your companions?"

8 "If you yourself do not know,
Most beautiful among women,
Go forth on the trail of the flock
And pasture your young goats
By the tents of the shepherds."

discussion questions

1. If you are engaged or married, what attracted you to your future spouse? If you are single, what do you consider "attractive?"

someone who loves Jesus
a leader
kind + sweet

2. According to these first eight verses, what attracts this man to this woman and this woman to this man?

Remember, if you're getting married for looks, when you get married, that's probably the most beautiful physically you're ever going to be in your life! It's all down hill after that!
~ Tommy Nelson

---

3. How does our society determine preparedness for marriage? Is there a grid? From what you learned in this session, when is someone ready to get married?

i think someone is ready when they are spiritually and financially ready to start a life together

4. We discover the woman working in the vineyards (v.5-6). Why is this signficant and what traits are revealed about her character?

UNPACKING THE TEXT

*"Your name is like **purified oil**."*

Pure oil was used in temple worship. This phrase signified a holy character– he was rightly related to God.

A man can't be a husband until he's been a bride. A man can't lead until a man follows...A man has to first submit to God.
~ *Tommy Nelson*

5. Why is mutual "respect" such a vital key to attraction?

Respect is a 2-way street

intentional intimacy

We may not admit it, but most of us either had or have a spouse checklist – that list of characteristics we want in a spouse. Let's take a look at that checklist.

Singles – How many items on your spouse checklist correlate with what we learned in this lesson about biblical attraction? Should you be making some changes to what you are looking for? Take a moment to write down your list and record what you have been looking for and also what you should be looking for. Maybe both lists have the same qualities listed - or maybe not. Maybe you need to reprioritize your list based on what we learned in this first session. Once you have reviewed (and/or revised) your list, share it with a trusted friend who can help you be accountable to look only for a mate that possesses these qualities. Commit to not compromise on this list just for the sake of settling or based on emotion.

_____

_____

_____

Married Couples – Your spouse checklist is probably long gone, but that doesn't mean that this topic is irrelevant. As you well know, your wedding day was only the beginning of marriage. The traits that you possess, and were attracted to, still need to be cultivated through the years. In all of the hustle and bustle of work, children, church – you name it – many of us can forget why we fell in love with our spouse. And it's easy to get tired (or lazy) and stop becoming the type of person we should be. So dust off your memory banks and write down the qualities that first attracted you to your spouse. Once you are done, switch lists with your spouse and ask them if you are still displaying these traits in your relationship. You might be surprised with what you find. Either way, you now have a tangible list of things to work on with your spouse.

_____

_____

_____

prayer requests

_____

_____

session two | the art of dating

Song of Solomon 1:9-2:7

I adjure you, O daughters of Jerusalem . . .that you not stir up or awaken love until it pleases.

*I*f sex could be compared to an apple pie, usually all that is left on most wedding days is the crust.

By the age of 16, virtually every teenager understands the intricacies, the dangers, and the details of how to drive a car, yet they remain clueless when it comes to the intricacies, dangers, and details of how to date a person.

Remember that first nervous touch? Maybe it was in a movie theater, on a couch, or a surreptitious brush under a table. The rapid heart beat. The short breaths. Sweat beading up on hands – and suddenly, the pinkies connect. Then THE question lurks into our hearts, "Now what?"

How far is too far in dating? Most people know all the reasons to "Just say no..." (STD's, guilt, and unplanned pregnancies). But if we place sex as the ultimate line, every person will tell you there is a risky minefield between hand holding and intercourse.

Without a map, especially as it relates to physical boundaries, it will be impossible to navigate the minefield of dating. One solution would be to kiss dating goodbye and totally shut oneself into a monastery. Should there be a place for dating in our society?

More importantly, how could a document written in a culture of arranged marriages enlighten our opinions on the 21st century phenomenon known as dating? The answers may surprise us...and just may guarantee that we have more than the crust on our wedding day.

gentle, kind

9 "To me, my darling, you are like
My mare among the chariots of Pharaoh."

10 "Your cheeks are lovely with ornaments,
Your neck with strings of beads."

11 "We will make for you ornaments of gold
With beads of silver."

12 "While the king was at his table,
My perfume gave forth its fragrance."

13 "My beloved is to me a pouch of myrrh
Which lies all night between my breasts."

14 "My beloved is to me a cluster of henna blossoms
In the vineyards of Engedi."

15 "How beautiful you are, my darling,
How beautiful you are!
Your eyes are like doves."

16 "How handsome you are, my beloved,
And so pleasant!
Indeed, our couch is luxuriant!"

17 "The beams of our houses are cedars,
Our rafters, cypresses."

2:1 "I am the rose of Sharon,
The lily of the valleys."

2 "Like a lily among the thorns,
So is my darling among the maidens."

3 "Like an apple tree among the trees of the forest,
So is my beloved among the young men.
In his shade I took great delight and sat down,
And his fruit was sweet to my taste."

4 "He has brought me to his banquet hall,
And his banner over me is love."

5 "Sustain me with raisin cakes,
Refresh me with apples,
Because I am lovesick."

6 "Let his left hand be under my head
And his right hand embrace me."

7 "I adjure you, O daughters of Jerusalem,
By the gazelles or by the hinds of the field,
That you do not arouse or awaken my love
Until she pleases."

discussion questions

1. How can expectations lead to struggles in a dating relationship?

Could lead to disappointment if expectations are unmet

2. In an old movie, a young man comes to ask a dad (Jimmy Stewart) for his daughter's hand in marriage. The young suitor asks, "Can I marry your daughter?" Jimmy Stewart's character replies, "Do you like her?" The young man replies, "Yes, sir, I love her." "No," the dad counters, "I didn't want to know that. I asked, 'Do you *like* her?'" Why is *liking* someone a necessary prerequisite to love?

being able to respect them and enjoy being around them, being their best friend
like their actions/character

> A date is nothing but an event between two people for edification and observation.
> ~ Tommy Nelson

3. The apostle Paul wrote in Romans, "Make no provision for the flesh, to fulfill its lusts" (13:14). We noticed this couple felt the same passions any young woman and man would feel, yet they remained pure. What are some practical safeguards dating couples can implement to keep them pure?

Stay away from places of temptation

4. If you are married with children, what are some practical ways you could teach these principles to your children before they get to the dating age?

self - worth

5. Everyone has had bad dating experiences. What are some lessons you've learned from the dating school of hard knocks?

UNPACKING THE TEXT

*Let's go out for some **raisin cakes**? (2:5)*

In the ancient near east, raisin cakes were considered to be aphrodisiacs. The raisins were considered to be "seeds" that could increase the "seed" of a couple so that conception was enhanced.

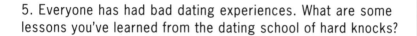

If you want to start a lasting fire, you're going to need some kindling and some serious firewood. The glowing coals of love, honesty, communication, and forgiveness take time to develop. They come from the firewood you gather over the course of discovering more about each other's character and relationship with God.

~ Tommy Nelson

intentional intimacy

Write down a few things that you look for in someone to date:

a leader and protector, someone who will love everything I am that God made me to be

When we first think of dating a person we naturally ask some questions:

Is he or she attractive?
Are they funny?
Do they like the same things I do?
What are their goals in life?

None of those questions is bad. But do you remember the illustration about the race presented at the end of this session? We need to find someone who is running spiritually at the same pace we are. Find out the *spiritual* pace of your potential spouse:

1. Does the person spend time daily with the Lord?
2. Is the person involved actively in a Christian church or other body of believers?
3. Does the person desire to pursue the same type of spiritual life and ministry that you desire to pursue?

Read some tips from Paul on dating: 1 Corinthians 6:18-20 and 2 Corinthians 6:14. What commitments can you make from these verses that will help you navigate the minefield of dating?

Married Couples – Realize these qualities are not simply for the dating years. They will be the glue that holds your marriage together during the hard times. Do you still have a quiet time? Are you still actively involved in church? Has your spiritual life deepened or dampened over the years?

prayer requests

3

session three | **the art of courtship, part I**

Song of Solomon 2:8-16

My beloved is mine, and I am his.

*C*ourtship. The very word sounds archaic. Antiquated. Passé.

In fact, courtship came from the Elizabethan era (remember Shakespeare?). Ladies waited for a suitor, either a knight or a lord, to win her hand through frequent visitation, gifts, and compliments. A man would ask the lady's father for permission to "court" his daughter. This implied that the man seriously and openly (in view of the royal court) desired to pursue the possibility of marriage. The father's permission allowed the suitor to express his love in the form of compliments. He could give the young lady trinkets of his affection and he could escort her to social events. If the two ever traveled away from the court, a chaperone was required.

Today, the thought of asking a father for permission to court, much less date his daughter is almost laughable. Rather than courting publicly, most young couples quickly seek privacy. With the advent of the automobile, the chaperone, along with chastity and sanctity, was left on the porch, and any couple suddenly had access to a mobile motel.

However, with the divorce rate among Christians hovering right around those of unbelievers and with more and more teens losing their virginity in the backseat, maybe it's time to reevaluate an antiquated practice. Maybe what is now considered passé deserves a second chance.

evaluation of stability

defining the relationship

courtship

8 "Listen! My beloved!
Behold, he is coming,
Climbing on the mountains,
Leaping on the hills!"

9 "My beloved is like a gazelle or a young stag.
Behold, he is standing behind our wall,
He is looking through the windows,
He is peering through the lattice."

① *desire should glow*
- courtship should be delightful

10 "My beloved responded and said to me,
'Arise, my darling, my beautiful one,
And come along.

11 'For behold, the winter is past,
The rain is over and gone.

12 'The flowers have already appeared in the land;
The time has arrived for pruning the vines,
And the voice of the turtledove has been heard in our land.

13 'The fig tree has ripened its figs,
And the vines in blossom have given forth their fragrance.
Arise, my darling, my beautiful one,
And come along!'"

14 "O my dove, in the clefts of the rock,

In the secret place of the steep pathway,

Let me see your form,

Let me hear your voice;

For your voice is sweet,

And your form is lovely."

She's taking her time

15 "Catch the foxes for us, *common commitement*

The little foxes that are ruining the vineyards,

While our vineyards are in blossom."

16 "My beloved is <u>mine</u>, and <u>I am his</u>; *She is secure*

He pastures his flock among the lilies." *her respect grows*

commitment

discussion questions

1. What is the difference between dating and courting?

2. At what point should a person be willing to call off the courtship? What would some indicators be that it's time to part ways?

3. Read verses 2:10-13. What is significant about the imagery here? How does this relate to courtship?

Courtship shouldn't be something you're fighting and breaking up and getting back together with and trying just to limp to the altar. There should be an easiness to that relationship.
~ Tommy Nelson

4. In our session on attraction, we discussed the importance of respect. In courtship, the key is *trust*. How is trust earned during this phase of the relationship and why is it so crucial to a marriage?

5. How does 2:14 reveal some differences between men and women? How does the woman respond to his advances in 2:16?

I am a strong believer in long dating, long courtship, and a brief engagement. Once the decision is made to marry, it is very difficult to restrain passion. Plan the wedding and get on with the marriage!
~ *Tommy Nelson*

6. Most scholars feel the "foxes" in 2:15 refer to sexual temptations that every couple encounters. Sexual passion will be a natural result of emotional intimacy. What are some practical steps to keeping the "foxes out of the vineyard?"

intentional intimacy

We tend to appreciate someone's unique gifts in dating and then find their weaknesses in marriage. Sometimes every relationship needs a reminder of why they chose to love in the first place.

Courtship is a great place to identify and appreciate your future spouse's gifts. Whether you are presently courting or have been hitched for twenty years, take a few moments to write down the gifts of your significant other. When you are finished, compare notes and write down the gifts your significant other listed for you. What did you learn from these lists?

Name: Gifts:	Name: Gifts:

Whether you are single or married, you need to construct "hedges" to protect yourself from the "foxes" of illicit sexual passion.

Singles – It is better to construct these hedges before courtship rather than during. Write down the commitments you will honor until you are married and find a trusted friend to hold you accountable.

Married Couples – Write down how you will keep the "little foxes" from creeping into your marriage.

prayer requests

_____
_____
_____
_____
_____

session four | **the art of courtship, part II**

Song of Solomon 2:17-3:11

Gaze on King Solomon on the day of his wedding, and on the day of his gladness of heart.

our words said it all. They appeared printed in bold type inside the store window of a Hollywood jewelry store:

> "WE RENT WEDDING RINGS."

Grocery store tabloids highlight all the glitzy, movie-star weddings. When was the last time you saw a 50th anniversary on one of those covers? Unfortunately, even beyond the media limelight, marriage has turned into a one-day event rather than a lifelong commitment.

Anyone can get married; few can sustain a marriage. Many who marry their "soul mate" end up three years later with a "roommate."

Where are you today? Nearlywed? Newlywed? Single or single again? Scratching the seven-year itch or celebrating thirty years of marital commitment? Regardless of your stage in life, if you have picked up this study guide, it's a safe bet you desire what God created in the heart of every man and woman: a desire for intimacy.

How you approach your wedding day will in many ways determine how you will stick together after your wedding day. Let's look at how Solomon "charged" down his wedding aisle and modeled the right start.

17 "Until the cool of the day when the shadows flee away,
Turn, my beloved, and be like a gazelle
Or a young stag on the mountains of Bether."

3:1 "On my bed night after night I sought him
Whom my soul loves;
I sought him but did not find him.

2 'I must arise now and go about the city;
In the streets and in the squares
I must seek him whom my soul loves.'
I sought him but did not find him."

3 "The watchmen who make the rounds in the city found me,
And I said, 'Have you seen him whom my soul loves?'

4 "Scarcely had I left them
When I found him whom my soul loves;
I held on to him and would not let him go
Until I had brought him to my mother's house,
And into the room of her who conceived me."

5 "I adjure you, O daughters of Jerusalem,
By the gazelles or by the hinds of the field,
That you will not arouse or awaken my love
Until she pleases."

6 "What is this coming up from the wilderness
Like columns of smoke,
Perfumed with myrrh and frankincense,
With all scented powders of the merchant?"

7 "Behold, it is the traveling couch of Solomon;
Sixty mighty men around it,
Of the mighty men of Israel."

8 "All of them are wielders of the sword,
Expert in war;
Each man has his sword at his side,
Guarding against the terrors of the night."

9 "King Solomon has made for himself a sedan chair
From the timber of Lebanon."

10 "He made its posts of silver,
Its back of gold
And its seat of purple fabric,
With its interior lovingly fitted out
By the daughters of Jerusalem."

11 "Go forth, O daughters of Zion,
And gaze on King Solomon with the crown
With which his mother has crowned him
On the day of his wedding,
And on the day of his gladness of heart."

discussion questions

1. Many people commit to a ban on the word "divorce" once they get married — meaning their vows are not optional. What other practical steps can a couple take to keep their promise to each other and to God?

communication

-pray together, both in God's word, praying for each other

2. What does Solomon's grand processional communicate to his bride? How is this beneficial to a woman as she approaches her wedding day?

-he will protect her (60 men)

-God brought them together

-she is safe

> *Have you ever seen a little boy with a G.I Joe with a tuxedo playing "wedding." A magazine rack with Grooms? Men are thinking about honeymoons, not about weddings!*
> ~ Tommy Nelson

3. Wedding days can be such a blur. How can a couple who has been married a long time bring back the magic of that day?

-the little things
-being thoughtful

4. If you are getting ready to be married, what spiritual symbols do you plan on using in your ceremony? Why are these significant?

UNPACKING THE TEXT

A central part of weddings in the Ancient Near East was the wedding processional. The groom would approach (3:6-10) his bride's house and take her to their new home. They would consummate the relationship and then there would be a seven day feast with family and friends.

The word sacrament means literally "sacred moment," and the sacrament of marriage is just that, the sacred moment of marriage. It is a moment in which God is fully present as the foremost witness to the wedding vows.
~ *Tommy Nelson*

5. If you are married, what symbols did you use in the wedding ceremony that had special significance to you as a couple? How have those symbols benefited your marriage?

intentional intimacy

Standing before the pastor, some couples repeat tried and true vows. Some are brave enough to write them personally and read them before their friends and family. Unfortunately, for most people, vows only make an appearance on the wedding day. Regardless of whether your vows were borrowed, original, or they have yet to be written, they were not intended just for one day.

They were meant for moments right after a bitter argument. They were intended for the long vigils beside a terminally ill spouse. They were crafted for a cruise celebrating 20 years of commitment. Vows should be displayed prominently, reflected on intentionally, and cherished permanently.

Where are your vows?
- Find your wedding vows and figure out a creative way to display them (framed, in your Daytimer™, or on your desk at work).

- If you have lost your wedding vows, go out on a special date with your spouse and rewrite them.

- If you are not yet married or are single again, give yourself an early wedding present by writing down the vows you want to say to your future spouse.

prayer requests

_____
_____
_____
_____
_____
_____
_____
_____
_____
_____

session five | **the art of intimacy, part I**

Song of Solomon 4:1-5:1

May my beloved come to his garden, and eat its choicest fruits.

*P*edal to the metal.

The young woman looks at her driver and brushes birdseed from his shoulders. The young man grips the steering wheel. He wipes a clammy hand on his tuxedo pants. He smiles at her. She glances in the mirror as she listens to the sound of empty soda cans clanging against the pavement. Her mind tries to catch glimpses of the previous four hours. His brain dreams about the next four hours. The needle speeds past 80.

He pulls into the parking lot, opens her door and takes her hand. As she exits the car her dress blossoms. They halt at the counter for a few nervous moments to grab the key. They approach the threshold door. His heart pushes through his shirt. She giggles and jumps into his arms. He carries her into oneness.

For some of you, that night brings back fond memories. For others, it may be a blurry vision of what is to come. While none of us would expose our honeymoon night to others, with this young couple in the Song of Solomon, God invites us to step into the bridal chamber.

4:1 "How beautiful you are, my darling,
How beautiful you are!
Your eyes are like doves behind your veil;
Your hair is like a flock of goats
That have descended from Mount Gilead."

2 "Your teeth are like a flock of newly shorn ewes
Which have come up from their washing,
All of which bear twins,
And not one among them has lost her young."

3 "Your lips are like a scarlet thread,
And your mouth is lovely.
Your temples are like a slice of a pomegranate
Behind your veil."

4 "Your neck is like the tower of David,
Built with rows of stones
On which are hung a thousand shields,
All the round shields of the mighty men."

5 "Your two breasts are like two fawns,
Twins of a gazelle
Which feed among the lilies."

6 "Until the cool of the day
When the shadows flee away,
I will go my way to the mountain of myrrh
And to the hill of frankincense."

7 "You are altogether beautiful, my darling,
And there is no blemish in you."

8 "Come with me from Lebanon, my bride,
May you come with me from Lebanon.
Journey down from the summit of Amana,
From the summit of Senir and Hermon,
From the dens of lions,
From the mountains of leopards."

9 "You have made my heart beat faster, my sister, my bride;
You have made my heart beat faster with a single glance of your eyes,
With a single strand of your necklace."

10 "How beautiful is your love, my sister, my bride!
How much better is your love than wine,
And the fragrance of your oils
Than all kinds of spices!"

11 "Your lips, my bride, drip honey;
Honey and milk are under your tongue,
And the fragrance of your garments is like the fragrance of Lebanon."

12 "A garden locked is my sister, my bride,
A rock garden locked, a spring sealed up."

13 "Your shoots are an orchard of pomegranates
With choice fruits, henna with nard plants,

14 Nard and saffron, calamus and cinnamon,
With all the trees of frankincense,
Myrrh and aloes, along with all the finest spices."

15 "You are a garden spring,
A well of fresh water,
And streams flowing from Lebanon."

16 "Awake, O north wind,
And come, wind of the south;
Make my garden breathe out fragrance,
Let its spices be wafted abroad.
May my beloved come into his garden
And eat its choice fruits!"

5:1 "I have come into my garden, my sister, my bride;
I have gathered my myrrh along with my balsam.
I have eaten my honeycomb and my honey;
I have drunk my wine and my milk.
Eat, friends;
Drink and imbibe deeply, O lovers."

_____

_____

_____

_____

_____

_____

_____

_____

_____

_____

_____

_____

_____

_____

_____

_____

_____

_____

_____

discussion questions

If you are in a small group, it may be beneficial to split into separate gender groups for this session.

1. What is unique about Solomon's approach to his bride compared to most men?

2. What fears did you have or do you have regarding your honeymoon? Was it or is it important to discuss expectations about the honeymoon? Why or why not?

> You have a God and no one can look upon Him and live. He is an invisible God. But the physical world that God made was something He made with design and purpose to be enjoyed. As a matter of fact, do you know what the term Eden is? It means delight. And so sex is a delightful thing to this couple.
> ~ *Tommy Nelson*

3. How was your honeymoon? Did it resemble this one? Why or why not?

4. What issues relating to sex are difficult to discuss with your spouse? What are some ways to open the conversation when it comes to sexual intimacy?

Great sex to a woman is tenderness. To a man, it's responsiveness. The couple had deeply met their mutual needs.
~ *Tommy Nelson*

5. How will your view of sexual intimacy change as a result of this chapter?

intentional intimacy

Honeymoons are great. But let's be honest, it's like trying on a new pair of shoes. Sometimes it takes a little while before you are totally comfortable. Unfortunately, due in large part to our church culture, we are never trained to intentionally talk about our sexual needs and issues with our spouse. One would think talking about it is a given, but for most couples, it's an experience to be enjoyed, but rarely discussed.

Whether you are fresh off your honeymoon, or flirting with your 25th anniversary, take a risk – talk about sex with your spouse or your future spouse. Be honest with your dreams, your hopes, your passions, and your desires. God meant for this most sacred act to be enjoyed. Enjoyment comes through greater knowledge of your needs and your spouse's needs.

Married Couples - Take a night out, or better yet, a weekend in a hotel room and ask some honest questions. After you are done, ask God to bless your physical intimacy. Then you might just want to light some candles and see where the night takes you.

Here are some questions:
- What do we love about our sex life?
- (Each ask) How can I serve and love you better when it comes to intimacy?
- Is there anything I do that bothers you or you wish I would do differently?
- What are some desires that you have for our physical intimacy?

Singles or Singles Again - There are many different things that are discussed in pre-marital counseling: finances, temperament, conflict, etc..., but one thing that is rarely discussed or only briefly mentioned on is sexual intimacy. Be committed to talking with your future spouse about your hopes, your passions, and your dreams as it relates to this most sacred and enjoyable act.

prayer requests

_____

_____

_____

_____

6

session six | the art of intimacy, part II

Until the cool of the day when the shadows flee away, I will go my way to the mountain of myrrh and to the hill of frankincense.

In our culture, sex sells everything from cars to carbonated drinks, from bran flakes to boats. Our society promotes sexuality as more fantasy than reality. If someone wanted to write a book about sex in marriage, the title might be *Great Expectations*.

Few areas in our marriage lug as much baggage as sex. Expectations are at an all time high. Husbands expect their wives to be Victoria's Secret models. Wives expect Casanova to sweep her off her feet. With such great expectations, both could end up being disappointed. At the same time, any meaningful conversation on the subject generally gets pushed aside by dishes, kids, work, and church events. It's easier just to pull the covers over the exasperation.

While the world creates great expectations based on fantasy; God created great expectations based on reality. The Author of sex knows exactly how it should be enjoyed – and He never meant for us to be in the dark. He desires for us to be fulfilled with our deepest sexual needs, not frustrated.

How is the intimacy in your marriage? Where are you in your sexual relationship? Fulfilled or frustrated? Are your expectations meeting reality? As a single, how are you dealing with your expectations? When you have honest questions, where do you turn for practical answers? Let the light of God's Word illuminate these intimate questions.

Principle #1
Understand the differences between men and women.

Principle #2
Understand my spouse's sexual needs.

Principle #3
Start early.

_____

_____

_____

_____

_____

_____

_____

_____

_____

_____

_____

_____

Principle #4

Read your spouse's signals.

Principle #5

Beware of combinations or predictability.

Principle #6

Beware of sexual boundaries of my mate.

_____

_____

_____

_____

_____

_____

_____

_____

_____

_____

_____

_____

discussion questions

Again, if you are in a small group, it may be beneficial to split into separate gender groups for this session.

1. Why is it so difficult to talk about sex within the church?

2. How did Tommy's points in this session impact you?

> *Men are microwaves, women are crock pots.*
> ~ Gary Smalley

3. What principle could impact your sex life now?

4. Just for fun, what is your signal to your spouse that you are ready for sexual intimacy?

I hope you're seeing the basis of great sex is friendship.
~ *Tommy Nelson*

5. Why does so much of sexual intimacy depend on friendship in marriage?

intentional intimacy

Below is a chart on the six principles for great sex. With each principle, write down some suggestions for your spouse. Be honest. Then go out for some coffee and discuss each of your suggestions and learn what your spouse suggests for you.

PRINCIPLE	SUGGESTION FOR MY SPOUSE	SUGGESTION FOR ME FROM MY SPOUSE
Understand the differences between men and women.		
Understand my spouse's sexual needs.		
Start early.		
Read your spouse's signals.		
Beware of combinations or predictability.		
Beware of the sexual boundaries of my mate.		

Singles - Find a trusted married friend of the same gender to discuss your expectations about sex.

prayer requests

_____

_____

_____

_____

session seven | **the art of conflict, part I**

Song of Solomon 5:2-6:10

My heart went out to him as he spoke. I searched for him but I did not find him; I called him but he did not answer me.

*W*hen was the last time your spouse hurt you? If you can't remember, then you're either just about to say, "I do," or you're living in denial. Two sinful people living under one roof can be a volatile mix. So, when was the last time you felt betrayed or slighted by your bride or groom? Was it an insult? A snide remark? A sarcastic comment about your cooking in front of friends? A constant nagging whenever you turn on the game? Or maybe you're dating or engaged and find yourself in an ongoing barrage of verbal barbs.

Now that you are thinking about how you didn't deserve to be treated with such callousness, think about how you responded. Did you return insult for insult? Did you hide the pain behind a veil of bitterness? Or did you find a way to "get even"?

Why do marriages turn into insult battlefields rather than blessing oases like you dreamt about and God intended? Most couples answer that question identically: "It's my spouse's fault. If I could just change them, my marriage would be great." But the Bible offers a much different solution.

2 "I was asleep but my heart was awake.
A voice! My beloved was knocking:
'Open to me, my sister, my darling,
My dove, my perfect one!
For my head is drenched with dew,
My locks with the damp of the night.'

3 "I have taken off my dress,
How can I put it on again?
I have washed my feet,
How can I dirty them again?"

4 "My beloved extended his hand through the opening,
And my feelings were aroused for him."

5 "I arose to open to my beloved;
And my hands dripped with myrrh,
And my fingers with liquid myrrh,
On the handles of the bolt."

6 "I opened to my beloved,
But my beloved had turned away and had gone!
My heart went out to him as he spoke.
I searched for him but I did not find him;
I called him but he did not answer me."

7 "The watchmen who make the rounds in the city found me,
They struck me and wounded me;
The guardsmen of the walls took away my shawl from me."

8 "I adjure you, O daughters of Jerusalem,
If you find my beloved,
As to what you will tell him:
For I am lovesick."

9 "What kind of beloved is your beloved,
O most beautiful among women?
What kind of beloved is your beloved,
That thus you adjure us?"

10 "My beloved is dazzling and ruddy,
Outstanding among ten thousand."

11 "His head is like gold, pure gold;
His locks are like clusters of dates
And black as a raven."

12 "His eyes are like doves
Beside streams of water,
Bathed in milk,
And reposed in their setting."

13 "His cheeks are like a bed of balsam,
Banks of sweet-scented herbs;
His lips are lilies
Dripping with liquid myrrh."

14 "His hands are rods of gold
Set with beryl;
His abdomen is carved ivory
Inlaid with sapphires."

15 "His legs are pillars of alabaster
Set on pedestals of pure gold;
His appearance is like Lebanon
Choice as the cedars."

16 "His mouth is full of sweetness.
And he is wholly desirable.
This is my beloved and this is my friend,
O daughters of Jerusalem."

6:1 "Where has your beloved gone,
O most beautiful among women?
Where has your beloved turned,
That we may seek him with you?"

2 "My beloved has gone down to his garden,
To the beds of balsam,
To pasture his flock in the gardens
And gather lilies."

3 "I am my beloved's and my beloved is mine,
He who pastures his flock among the lilies."

4 "You are as beautiful as Tirzah, my darling,
As lovely as Jerusalem,
As awesome as an army with banners."

5 "Turn your eyes away from me,
For they have confused me;
Your hair is like a flock of goats
That have descended from Gilead."

6 "Your teeth are like a flock of ewes
Which have come up from their washing,
All of which bear twins,
And not one among them has lost her young."

7 "Your temples are like a slice of a pomegranate
Behind your veil."

8 "There are sixty queens and eighty concubines,
And maidens without number;

9 But my dove, my perfect one, is unique:
She is her mother's only daughter;
She is the pure child of the one who bore her.
The maidens saw her and called her blessed,
The queens and the concubines also, and they
  praised her, saying,

10 'Who is this that grows like the dawn,
As beautiful as the full moon,
As pure as the sun,
As awesome as an army with banners?'"

discussion questions

1. What are typical things that bring conflict in marriage or in relationships?

2. How do you "react" to your mate? For some it may be the silent treatment, for others, it's like tripping a land mine. What are some unhealthy ways you've reacted to your mate in the past?

> *Express yourself, yes, but wait until your emotional temperature has cooled. Wait until the one who has hurt you also has cooled off or is in a good frame of mind to hear what you have to say.*
> ~ *Tommy Nelson*

3. Our natural response to any offense is to retaliate and seek revenge. Is that biblical? Look up 1 Thessalonians 5:15 and 1 Peter 2:21-25, how can these verses apply to marital conflict?

4. Has nagging ever helped transform a person? Why do we resort to nagging our spouses? From today's lesson, what is the best way to seek transformation in our spouse?

UNPACKING THE TEXT

*"His eyes are like white doves . . . and **fitly set**"* (5:12)

When Solomon's bride tells him his eyes are "fitly set," she means they were wide and focused on her. He did not have a shifty gaze of mistrust, nor were his eyes openly flared in anger. They were eyes of faithfulness and kindness.

Seven Communication Tips:
1. **Listen with your face**
2. **Don't reason with your mate**
3. **Don't argue**
4. **Don't interrupt**
5. **Don't stomp out the door**
6. **Don't vent your "spleen" to others**
7. **Don't use rude body language**

5. Have you noticed traits in your spouse that you appreciate even more as a result of conflict? What are they?

intentional intimacy

One of the most practical verses in all of Scripture is Ephesians 4:26:

"Be angry, and yet do not sin; do not let the sun go down on your anger."

Notice that it does not say, "don't ever get angry." The Bible says, in our anger, don't sin. Our spouses will hurt us and we will hurt them. Often times these hurts may lead to anger. But if we respond with agape love rather than retaliation, we can move towards resolution rather than revenge.

Also, you will see that we are never to go to bed mad. This doesn't mean, "stay up and fight!" This means that we should seek a resolution quickly rather than letting unresolved anger fester. If resolution needs more time, schedule a time to talk more the following day.

Are there opportunities for you to actively apply agape love in your marriage right now? Instead of hunkering down in bitterness, why not find a way to bless your spouse before you turn out the light? Here are some steps for resolution:

1. Seek forgiveness from God for any anger or bitterness that is in your own heart.
2. Affirm your commitment and love for your spouse verbally.
3. Take "always" and "never" out of your vocabulary. Make the object of your discussion a specific situation where you were hurt rather than your spouse. For example, rather than saying, "You never make me feel special," say, "It has been a couple of weeks since you and I had time alone, it has made me feel as if you don't value me."
4. Come to a unified resolution.
5. Pray together for renewed commitment.

Singles - These habits of good conflict resolution will transfer into a marriage relationship. As you examine your friendships, are you allowing bitterness to build up with anyone? Are there any relationships you need to mend?

prayer requests

_____

_____

_____

8

session eight | the art of conflict, part II

Song of Solomon 6:11-13

Come back, come back, O Shulammite; Come back, come back, that we may gaze at you!

here are usually three stages to marriage. The first is the honeymoon. Honeymoon literally means, "sweet month." Then you go to the next stage – disillusionment. You thought you married Mr. or Mrs. Perfect, but soon you discovered that both you and your spouse have a few flaws to work through. Maybe they don't put the toilet paper on the right way, forgot how to pick up their clothes, or just have this "unique" habit you never noticed before. Nothing too traumatic, just differences that take some getting used to in those first years together.

Then you move to the final stage – commitment. You discover your mate all over again and you commit to love them in a biblical manner. Part of that commitment is learning to fight clean and resolve conflict. If you don't have conflict in your marriage, more than likely you are a maid married to a butler. You perform functions, but have no intimacy. Or one person has waved the white flag of surrender and buried their pain in the bunker of their heart. Marriages without conflict are not healthy marriages.

The point is all couples fight. Good couples fight clean. Bad couples fight dirty. Good couples press to a resolution. Bad couples press for a victory. When one person wins, both lose. For good couples, a conflict will expose character. For bad couples a conflict will expose immaturity. Most couples have a track record of conflict, but they don't have a good track record of resolution.

While conflict is inevitable, resolution must be intentional. Whether you are single or married, relationships will flounder or flourish based upon your ability to resolve conflict. How can we move from wounding our spouse to healing our spouse? How can we move from irritation to intimacy? Fortunately God doesn't leave us wondering. He's offered a proven plan for resolution.

11 "I went down to the orchard of nut trees
To see the blossoms of the valley,
To see whether the vine had budded
Or the pomegranates had bloomed."

12 "Before I was aware, my soul set me
Over the chariots of my noble people."

13 "Come back, come back, O Shulammite;
Come back, come back, that we may gaze at you!"
Why should you gaze at the Shulammite,
As at the dance of the two companies?

discussion questions

1. Most marriage conflicts tend to arise from: (1) a failure of communication, (2) financial difficulties, (3) sexual difficulties, (4) problems with in-laws, or (5) disagreements about child rearing. Which conflict has been the most difficult to discuss in your marriage and why?

2. Can people ever truly "forget" a wrong? What are some practical ways we can forgive and not hold grudges?

Resolution is not automatic. It doesn't happen over time or by accident. For a conflict to be resolved, there must be an intentional desire for reconciliation followed by action. Resolution requires effort, time, and a certain degree of skill.
~ *Tommy Nelson*

3. Can you give an example where a conflict has deepened your love for your spouse?

4. Of the principles of resolution from this session, which one(s) do you generally practice well?

5. Now the flip side. Which one(s) are the hardest to practice in the midst of conflict?

> Don't react to your mate. Let God do the chastening. Resolve that we're going to change whatever we have to, to maintain our happiness and our union. You talk. The offender says, "I'm sorry." The offended says, "I forgive you and I'm going to forget it." Then we're going to dance. We get deeper. That's resolution.
> ~ Tommy Nelson

6. Have you ever witnessed a couple model good resolution skills? If so, tell the group about a specific conflict that was resolved well.

intentional intimacy

Here's a review of the principles of resolution:

> **The 17 "Nevers" of Communicating with Your Spouse**
>
> 1. Never raise your voice in your home.
> 2. Never publicly embarrass your mate.
> 3. Never quarrel before the children.
> 4. Never use the kids to win an argument.
> 5. Never talk about your spouse outside of your marriage.
> 6. Never use sex to win.
> 7. Never touch in anger.
> 8. Never call names.
> 9. Never get historical and call into account a wrong suffered.
> 10. Never stomp out.
> 11. Never freeze your mate out.
> 12. Never use the in-laws.
> 13. Never reason in the face of pain.
> 14. Never let the sun go down on your wrath and give the devil an opportunity.
> 15. Never reverse an argument.
> 16. Never fail to listen to your mate.
> 17. Never harden yourself towards your spouse.

Take a night out with your spouse and this study guide. Let each other know which principles you are applying well. Then talk about the two or three principles that need improving. When you are done, write out a covenant to each other:

I,_____,commit to _____

_____

during the course of a conflict. Further, I make resolution, not victory, my number one goal whenever conflict arises.

I,_____,commit to _____

_____

during the course of a conflict. Further, I make resolution, not victory, my number one goal whenever conflict arises.

prayer requests

_____

session nine | the art of romance, part I

Song of Solomon 7:1-13

The mandrakes have given forth fragrance; and over our doors are all choice fruits, both new and old, which I have saved up for you, my beloved.

*M*arriages begin warm and intimate but over time they can become cold and businesslike. Consider how the treatments change over the years with a "marriage cold":

The first year the husband says: "Sugar, I'm worried about my precious bride. You've got a bad sniffle. I want to put you in the hospital for a complete check-up. I know the food is lousy, but I've arranged for your meals to be sent up from Rossini's. It's all arranged."

The second year: "Listen honey, I don't like the sound of that cough. I've called Dr. Miller and he's going to rush right over. Now will you go to bed like a good girl for me, please?"

The third year: "Maybe you'd better lie down, honey. Nothing like a little rest if you're feeling bad. I'll bring you something to eat. Have we got any soup in the house?"

The fourth year: "Look dear. Be sensible. After you've fed the kids and washed the dishes you'd better hit the sack."

The fifth year: "Why don't you take a couple of aspirin?"

The sixth year: "If you'd just gargle or something, instead of sitting around barking like a seal."

The seventh year: "For heaven's sake, stop sneezing. What are you trying to do, give me pneumonia?"

While the story is funny, the reality can be painful. Many walk down the aisle with their soul-mate, but end up with a roommate. Romance before marriage flamed up like a blazing forest fire, but for some, romance after marriage barely flickers.

No matter the size of the bonfire, left untended it will burn out. A fire needs fuel. Once the adrenaline, mystery, and infatuation runs out, what fuel will sustain your love? God never intended years of marriage to pour water on the flames of romance. In fact, rather than dampen, He intended romance to deepen as the years pass.

7:1 "How beautiful are your feet in sandals,
O prince's daughter!
The curves of your hips are like jewels,
The work of the hands of an artist."

2 "Your navel is like a round goblet
Which never lacks mixed wine;
Your belly is like a heap of wheat
Fenced about with lilies."

3 "Your two breasts are like two fawns,
Twins of a gazelle."

4 "Your neck is like a tower of ivory,
Your eyes like the pools in Heshbon
By the gate of Bath-rabbim;
Your nose is like the tower of Lebanon,
Which faces toward Damascus."

5 "Your head crowns you like Carmel,
And the flowing locks of your head are like purple threads;
The king is captivated by your tresses."

6 "How beautiful and how delightful you are,
My love, with all your charms!"

7 "Your stature is like a palm tree,
And your breasts are like its clusters."

8 "I said, 'I will climb the palm tree,
I will take hold of its fruit stalks.'
Oh, may your breasts be like clusters of the vine,
And the fragrance of your breath like apples,

9 And your mouth like the best wine!"
It goes down smoothly for my beloved,
Flowing gently through the lips of those who fall asleep.

10 "I am my beloved's,
And his desire is for me."

11 "Come, my beloved, let us go out into the country,
Let us spend the night in the villages."

12 "Let us rise early and go to the vineyards;
Let us see whether the vine has budded
And its blossoms have opened,
And whether the pomegranates have bloomed.
There I will give you my love."

13 "The mandrakes have given forth fragrance;
And over our doors are all choice fruits,
Both new and old,
Which I have saved up for you, my beloved.

discussion questions

1. What can hinder romance in marriage?

2. Throughout the book, we notice the husband often communicates appreciation to his wife. What principles can we draw from this as it relates to deepening romance?

> Husbands, you can be romantic. God desires for you to be romantic, and it's up to you to take the lead in romance in your marriage. Early on it was your *instinct* to be romantic. Later, it must become a *discipline*.
> ~ Tommy Nelson

3. Romance needs "emotional nourishment". What you feed your spouse is likely to be what you are fed in return. What are ways you can help your spouse understand your emotional cravings?

4. Proverbs 31:31 says, "Give her the fruit of her hands." He means that wives should be praised by their husbands. Wives, what are ways you like to be affirmed by your husband? Husbands, what ways do you currently affirm your wife?

UNPACKING THE TEXT

In 7:4, "Your nose is like the **tower of Lebanon**."

The tower of Lebanon faced toward Damascus. That's where the enemies would attack Israel. The tower of Lebanon was national defense and security. He is saying to his wife "your face always faces the enemy." This woman was faithful to this man and to God. She wouldn't let anything stain the reputation of either.

> The way a woman spells love over time is tenderness. The way a man spells love over time is respect.
> ~ Tommy Nelson

5. One way to deepen romance is to acknowledge the best in your spouse. Right now, look at your spouse and say a few things that you deeply appreciate about him or her.

intentional intimacy

Plan a surprise romantic getaway for your spouse. Plan every detail, from the itinerary to the babysitter. It could be simple or elaborate; expensive or economical; but make it creative and meaningful. Here are some ideas:

- Go back to the place you had your first date and talk about all the reasons why you fell in love.
- Take a cruise for a special anniversary.
- Send your wife to an all-day spa; meet her at her favorite restaurant.
- Send a note to your husband at work, "Meet me at the Hilton, room 323."
- Hide love letters at work or home for your spouse to find.

Whatever you do, remember, romance will die if left untended. It takes intentionality to keep the home fires burning.

prayer requests

_____

_____

_____

_____

_____

_____

_____

session ten | **the art of romance, part II**

Song of Solomon 8:1-4

Let his left hand be under my head and his right hand embrace me.

movie opened with the lead character saying these words, "I am 66 years old. I am recently retired. Helen and I have been married 42 years. Lately I find myself asking the same question, 'Who is this old woman who lives in my house.'"

Where will your marriage be 5, 10, 20, or 42 years from now?

- *Intimate friends or casual roommates?*
- *Will the best memories be long behind you or in front of you?*
- *Will television replace conversation?*
- *Will all your deep discussions center on your kids?*

In the last chapter we discussed how God intended romance to deepen rather than dampen over the year. Yet we all know it's easy to let the urgent push out the necessary. It's easy to let the clamor of kids drown out conversation. It's easy to let meetings fill the Daytimer™ spots where dates once stood.

Habits will form in our marriages because of intention or inattention. In this lesson we are going to discover some practical and simple principles that will help us fuel the fires of our passion. It sounds like honeymooner's idealism, but God desires the forty-second year of marriage to be as rich as the first.

8:1 "Oh that you were like a brother to me
Who nursed at my mother's breasts.
If I found you outdoors, I would kiss you;
No one would despise me, either."

2 "I would lead you and bring you
Into the house of my mother, who used to instruct me;
I would give you spiced wine to drink from the juice of my
pomegranates."

3 "Let his left hand be under my head
And his right hand embrace me."

4 "I want you to swear, O daughters of Jerusalem,
Do not arouse or awaken my love
Until she pleases."

_____

_____

_____

_____

_____

_____

_____

_____

_____

_____

_____

_____

_____

_____

_____

_____

_____

_____

_____

_____

discussion questions

1. Share an unexpected romantic moment from your marriage.

2. What are some practical ways to keep the "chores" of daily life from infringing upon the spontaneity of romance?

> *A noted radio personality said that to her, "The sound of her husband vacuuming the house is foreplay."*
> ~ Tommy Nelson

The Six E's of an Affair

1. Elimination
2. Encounter
3. Enjoyment
4. Expedition
5. Expression
6. Experience

3. In this session in the curriculum, Tommy Nelson discussed the six steps to an affair. This is not a formula, but a strong warning on how to recognize the steps that lead to one so that they can be avoided. What are some practical ways to guard against a spouse inadvertently getting their needs met outside of marriage?

Whether you are married, or single, commit now to protect yourself from these temptations.

4. How would you describe an ideal date with your spouse? In what ways do you keep date nights from becoming routine?

Let a husband fulfill his duty to his wife, the wife to her husband. There are needs that we need to be sensitive to meet in each other because Satan will supply that need if it's not met by our mates.
~ *Tommy Nelson*

5. What couple you know has modeled a romantic marriage over a long period of time? How did they exhibit their love? What traits would you hope to emulate in your own marriage?

intentional intimacy

1 Peter 3:7 states, "You husbands in the same way, live with your wives in an understanding way, as with someone weaker, since she is a woman; and show her honor as a fellow heir of the grace of life, so that your prayers will not be hindered."

Another way to translate "understanding way" is "according to knowledge." Peter exhorts the husband to be a student of his wife. You want to be insightful when it comes to your spouse. We should love our spouse according to their love language, not ours.

In the space below, write down the ways that you most often try to love your spouse and the ways you want to be loved. These may be acts of service or words of encouragement or anything that you perceive as loving you or you loving your spouse.

_____

_____

_____

Now compare your list with your spouse. How are you doing? How are they doing? Are there ways that you both want to be loved that you individually are not meeting? Do you express love to your spouse in ways that are not necessarily important to them? How can you adjust your expressions of love so that your spouse's needs will be met? How can they adjust as well to meet your needs? Be open and honest with this discussion and use the lines below to record steps you can both take to meet each other's needs.

_____

_____

_____

prayer requests

_____

_____

_____

_____

session eleven | **the art of commitment**

Song of Solomon 8:5-14

Many waters cannot quench love, nor will rivers overflow it; if a man were to give all the riches of his house for love, it would be utterly despised.

$\mathcal{S}$omeone once said, "When you get married, you get measured for your tux and your coffin at the same time." God's intention from the Garden was one man for one woman for one lifetime. We marry for life, we are parted by death. However, looking at our cultural landscape, it appears "until death do us part" is more of a catch phrase than a fervent covenant.

With 35% of marriages (both Christian and non-Christian[1]) ending in divorce, we must ask, "How can anyone stay faithful to their spouse?"

Marriage wasn't simply a nice idea from God. He began and ended His Word with a marriage. He chose a man married to a woman as the fundamental building blocks of society. In the Old Testament, God was called the Husband of Israel. In the New Testament, Paul chose marriage as the symbol for the union between Christ and the Church. God's faithfulness to man is pictured with the faithfulness of one man to one woman for one lifetime.

There are some people going through this study who have experienced a divorce. If so, you are not second-class in God's eyes. He cleanses us from all our sins, guilt, and shame (1 John 4:4) and only asks that we start fresh with the truth we have learned.

As we close our study, we are going to discover how the "essence of love" will provide a clue for remaining faithful in marriage. While sexual passion is a theme of the Song of Solomon, we also discover that a life-long commitment is too...from the tux to the coffin.

---

[1] Barna, George. "Born Again Christians Just as Likely to Divorce as are Non-Christians," Sept. 8, 2004, from www.barna.org; accessed on April 12, 2005.

5 "Who is this coming up from the wilderness
Leaning on her beloved?"
Beneath the apple tree I awakened you;
There your mother was in labor with you,
There she was in labor and gave you birth."

6 "Put me like a seal over your heart,
Like a seal on your arm.
For love is as strong as death,
Jealousy is as severe as Sheol;
Its flashes are flashes of fire,
The very flame of the Lord."

7 "Many waters cannot quench love,
Nor will rivers overflow it;
If a man were to give all the riches of his house for love,
It would be utterly despised."

8 "We have a little sister,
And she has no breasts;
What shall we do for our sister
On the day when she is spoken for?"

9 "If she is a wall,
We will build on her a battlement of silver;
But if she is a door,
We will barricade her with planks of cedar."

10 "I was a wall, and my breasts were like towers;
Then I became in his eyes as one who finds peace."

11 "Solomon had a vineyard at Baal-hamon;
He entrusted the vineyard to caretakers.
Each one was to bring a thousand shekels of silver
 for its fruit."

12 "My very own vineyard is at my disposal;
The thousand shekels are for you, Solomon,
And two hundred are for those who take care of its fruit."

13 "O you who sit in the gardens,
My companions are listening for your voice,
Let me hear it!"

14 "Hurry, my beloved,
And be like a gazelle or a young stag
On the mountains of spices."

discussion questions

1. How has our culture taken for granted the phrase, "til death do us part?" How can couples regain the sanctity of the marriage covenant?

2. In verse 8:6, is "jealousy" viewed as a positive trait in marriage? If so, how?

> **Marriage is not a temporary driving permit for a spin down life's highway. It is a permanent state of being.**
> ~ *Tommy Nelson*

3. Why is purity before marriage such a key component to faithfulness during marriage?

4. In this session in the curriculum, Tommy Nelson talked about the "essence of love" being service? How has this played out in your marriage? What ways can you serve your spouse that you may have neglected over time?

5. Do you believe that it's true that marriage is like a triangle – the closer each spouse gets to God, the closer they get to each other? How have you seen that work in your marriage?

> At every conference there are always several people that come to a recognition that marriage is a divine institution and the reason that we're having problems in marriage is that individually we're having problems with God.
> ~ *Tommy Nelson*

6. Many people in our culture either come from a divorced family or are divorced themselves. How do you start over with the right perspective on marriage?

intentional intimacy

For your last activity, take a few moments to read back through this study guide. Look at how God has impacted your life through the Song of Solomon. In the space below write down the insights you have applied or want to apply to your marriage (or future marriage).

_____

_____

_____

_____

_____

Married Couples - Take some time to pray for your marriage with your spouse. Ask God to help you keep service to each other as the "essence of love." Pray that God may keep you faithful to each other until He calls you home.

Singles - Pray now for your future spouse and marriage. Commit to the Lord today that you will never settle for anything other than God's best. Pick a close friend or family member who will keep you accountable to the standards you have set for yourself and your future marriage and share with them your commitment.

prayer requests

_____

_____

_____

_____

_____

_____

_____

We are all in relationships. *But there is no one on earth who can meet all of our needs.*

God designed relationships that way. He never intended friendships or marriage to fill the deepest longings of our heart – that space was reserved only for Him. Our relationships, especially our marriages, will only deepen if we are first connected with our Creator. Even if we could apply every principle in this study guide, without the person of Jesus Christ in our lives, something would still be missing.

God created you to have a relationship with Him. However, in order to have that relationship, God set a standard - perfection. *"For all have sinned and fall short of the Glory of God"* (Romans 3:23). We all have fallen short of God's standard and lived independently of God. Fortunately, Jesus Christ lived a perfect life and died on a cross in our place for our sins (Romans 5:8). When Jesus rose from the dead, He made it possible for anyone to enter a personal relationship with God through salvation in Jesus Christ (Romans 10:9-10).

Romans 6:23 states, *"...but the gift of God is eternal life through Jesus Christ our Lord."* No matter how many times you have messed up or sinned, God desires to forgive you and set you on a new path (Ephesians 2:8-9). Ask Him to forgive you, and then place your trust in His Son Jesus Christ, our Savior (Romans 10:13). God is all about new beginnings.

God does not love you because you are perfect, because you are not. *He loves you because He sees you through His Son's perfection.* At any time you can come before God with a humble heart and He will renew your heart and give you hope for all your relationships. **From friendships to marriage, your relationships will never be all they were intended to be without the person of Jesus Christ in your life.**

steps to **grow in Christ**:

- *If you are not already, get involved in a local church that preaches God's Word as applicable to all areas of life.*

- *Ask a pastor or teacher to help you start reading the Bible for yourself.*

- *Get involved in a small group or find a group of friends to which you can be accountable as you grow in Christ.*

In the following pages, we have included the complete text from the Song of Solomon with notes and personal observations from Tommy Nelson. Because Tommy originally developed this material and is featured in the curriculum, we hope you find his thoughts on each chapter useful in your own study of this book.

a note from tommy:
on his Bible study methods.

tommy nelson

EVERY YEAR I TRY TO GO THROUGH MY BIBLE ANEW. I MAKE OBSERVATIONS OF THE TEXT WITHIN THE VERSES AND THEN OBSERVE BETWEEN THE VERSES. I LOOK FOR THE FLOW OF THE TEXT AND THE DEVELOPMENT OF THE BIBLICAL IDEAS. I TRY TO SPOT KEY WORDS, COMPARISONS ("LIKE" OR "AS"), CONTRASTS ("BUT" AND "HOWEVER"), EXPLANATIONS ("FOR" AND "BECAUSE"), REPETITIONS, SYNONYMS, AND - ESPECIALLY IN THIS BOOK - METAPHORS.

I ALSO LOOK FOR THE USE OF INTERROGA- TION OR QUESTIONS TO RAISE AN ISSUE THAT THE READER IS MEANT TO ANSWER. AND FROM A BIRDS-EYE VIEW I WANT TO WATCH THE GIVE AND TAKE BETWEEN SOLOMON AND THE WOMAN. IN FACT, THIS IS THE KEY TO THE SONG OF SOLOMON... THE DEVELOPMENT OF A RELATIONSHIP AND THE STANDARD OF HOW A COUPLE INTERACTS.

THROUGH THE YEARS, I HAVE BENEFITTED FROM THE TRAINING OF PROFESSORS AND TEACHERS AND I HOPE THAT A LOOK AT THESE NOTES WILL HELP AS YOU STUDY THE BIBLE. THEY WILL ALSO GIVE YOU A GLIMPSE OF HOW I HAVE DEVELOPED THIS SERIES ON SONG OF SOLOMON.

Tommy Nelson

Attraction

Solomon wrote over 1000 songs
(1 kgs 4:32) as well as a
number of Psalms..
Two of his Psalms dealt with
weddings (Ps.

He is Physically delightful ————

His character is pure or holy ————

He was popular ————

She considers herself privileged ————
to be his wife..

.. in the intimacy of his home ————

The "daughters of Jerusalem"
a kind of chorus that asks her
questions that develop the
Narrative. They declare Solomon worthy

After the man's character is ————
highlighted, now the woman's

She too is physically attractive but
character surpasses looks

1.
She is hardworking.. a servant

1.E. her brothers ————
2.
She is obedient to authority ————

her Physical appearance

1 The Song of Songs, which is Solomon's.

2 "May he kiss me with the kisses of his mouth!
For your love is better than wine."

3 "Your oils have a pleasing fragrance,
Your name is like purified oil;
Therefore the maidens love you."

4 "Draw me after you and let us run together!
The king has brought me into his chambers.
We will rejoice in you and be glad;
We will extol your love more than wine.
Rightly do they love you."

5 "I am black but lovely,
O daughters of Jerusalem,
Like the tents of Kedar,
Like the curtains of Solomon."

6 "Do not stare at me because I am swarthy,
For the sun has burned me.
My mother's sons were angry with me;
They made me caretaker of the vineyards,
But I have not taken care of my own vineyard."

7"Tell me, O you whom my soul loves,

Where do you pasture your flock,

Where do you make it lie down at noon?

For why should I be like one who veils herself

Beside the flocks of your companions?"

8 "If you yourself do not know,

Most beautiful among women,

Go forth on the trail of the flock

And pasture your young goats

By the tents of the shepherds."

3 She is morally upright.
Committed to Purity.

the Prostitutes (Gen. 38:15)
who veiled themselves.
She will meet a man in the light not in
the darkness of sin

She is encouraged to seek such a man by
the daughters of Jerusalem

DATING
The couple eats together
twice v.12, 2:4
(and possibly 1:16)
He is gentle with her
He compliments her

9 "To me, my darling, you are like
My mare among the chariots of Pharaoh."

10 "Your cheeks are lovely with ornaments,
Your neck with strings of beads."

11 "We will make for you ornaments of gold
With beads of silver."

He edifies her. He is her beauty.
~~loveliness~~ loveliness

12 "While the king was at his table,
My perfume gave forth its fragrance."

i.e. his memory is pleasant
on her heart.

13 "My beloved is to me a pouch of myrrh
Which lies all night between my breasts."

He is sweet

14 "My beloved is to me a cluster of henna blossoms
In the vineyards of Engedi."

15 "How beautiful you are, my darling,
How beautiful you are!
Your eyes are like doves."

There is definite Physical
Attraction...
But note that it is after they are
Spiritually.. Socially on solid
footing.

16 "How handsome you are, my beloved,
And so pleasant!
Indeed, our couch is luxuriant!"

There is Propriety
They are in the open
In the light

17 "The beams of our houses are cedars,
Our rafters, cypresses."

2:1 "I am the rose of Sharon,
The lily of the valleys."

*She Grows in her Perception of herself
(compare 1:5)*

2 "Like a lily among the thorns,
So is my darling among the maidens."

He doesn't lead her on and flit from one Girl to the other.

3 "Like an apple tree among the trees of the forest,
So is my beloved among the young men.
In his shade I took great delight and sat down,
And his fruit was sweet to my taste."

She Grows in Respect

*He Protects her
and nourishes her*

4 "He has brought me to his banquet hall,
And his banner over me is love."

He honors her Publically

a term of ownership

5 "Sustain me with raisin cakes,
Refresh me with apples,
Because I am lovesick."

She is Passionate in how she feels about him...

6 "Let his left hand be under my head
And his right hand embrace me."

a longing for Physical intimacy

7 "I adjure you, O daughters of Jerusalem,
By the gazelles or by the hinds of the field,
That you do not arouse or awaken my love
Until she pleases."

The man Responds to her Passion with Protection and Self-control.

i.e true for all women

a term of Gentleness (Prov. 5:19)

More literally "do not arouse or awaken love until it pleases"

" There is a time and Place for intimacy... but its not now "

Courtship

She is a "doe" and he is the "stag" in springtime (vv 10-13). It is becoming the "time" for love to awaken.

Their excitement grows.

he gets closer and closer

He invites her to come with him

Springtime. The time of new life. Such should be a deepening love.

8 "Listen! My beloved!
Behold, he is coming,
Climbing on the mountains,
Leaping on the hills!"

9 "My beloved is like a gazelle or a young stag.
Behold, he is standing behind our wall,
He is looking through the windows,
He is peering through the lattice."

10 "My beloved responded and said to me,
'Arise, my darling, my beautiful one,
And come along.

11 'For behold, the winter is past,
The rain is over and gone.

12 'The flowers have already appeared in the land;
The time has arrived for pruning the vines,
And the voice of the turtledove has been heard in our land.

13 'The fig tree has ripened its figs,
And the vines in blossom have given forth their fragrance.
'Arise, my darling, my beautiful one,
And come along!'"

14 "O my dove, in the clefts of the rock,

In the secret place of the steep pathway,

Let me see your form,

Let me hear your voice;

For your voice is sweet,

And your form is lovely."

15 "Catch the foxes for us,

The little foxes that are ruining the vineyards,

While our vineyards are in blossom."

16 "My beloved is mine, and I am his;

He pastures his flock among the lilies."

Handwritten annotations:

She is Reticent. She is in a protected Place.

He assures her of his delight in her and asks her to trust him

Their trust has deepened

a Joint-commitment

The Relationship is Pictured as a Vineyard. They are committed to Protecting it from the "little foxes" that cause it not to mature.

as a Result She Grows in Security and Respect

morningtime when the darkness lifts

She longs for her young "stag" to be upon her "2 hills" (Bether is Hebrew for "separation") It speaks of the womans breasts

She longs for him at nite —

(Some hold that 3:1-4 is her recurring Dream of Longing) She goes to look for him

17 "Until the cool of the day when the shadows flee away,

Turn, my beloved, and be like a gazelle

Or a young stag on the mountains of Bether."

3:1 "On my bed night after night I sought him

Whom my soul loves;

I sought him but did not find him.

2 'I must arise now and go about the city;

In the streets and in the squares

I must seek him whom my soul loves.'

I sought him but did not find him."

3 "The watchmen who make the rounds in the city found me,

And I said, 'Have you seen him whom my soul loves?'

4 "Scarcely had I left them

When I found him whom my soul loves;

I held on to him and would not let him go

Until I had brought him to my mother's house,

And into the room of her who conceived me."

She introduces him to her mother, hastening the wedding day...

Again Solomon urges her to wait for the right time to awaken love.

5 "I adjure you, O daughters of Jerusalem,

By the gazelles or by the hinds of the field,

That you will not arouse or awaken my love

Until she pleases."

6 "What is this coming up from the wilderness
Like columns of smoke,
Perfumed with myrrh and frankincense,
With all scented powders of the merchant?"

The Wedding
He is coming for her
..in Regal splendor..

7 "Behold, it is the traveling couch of Solomon;
Sixty mighty men around it,
Of the mighty men of Israel."

She is safe with him

8 "All of them are wielders of the sword,
Expert in war;
Each man has his sword at his side,
Guarding against the terrors of the night."

9 "King Solomon has made for himself a sedan chair
From the timber of Lebanon."

..secure and solid..

10 "He made its posts of silver,
Its back of gold
And its seat of purple fabric,
With its interior lovingly fitted out
By the daughters of Jerusalem."

..wealthy..
..and beautiful..

11 "Go forth, O daughters of Zion,
And gaze on King Solomon with the crown
With which his mother has crowned him
On the day of his wedding,
And on the day of his gladness of heart."

He is the true King

The Honeymoon

Solomon praises her from "head to toe"...

her WEDDING veil —

Soft, descending downward —

4:1 "How beautiful you are, my darling,
How beautiful you are!
Your eyes are like doves behind your veil;
Your hair is like a flock of goats
That have descended from Mount Gilead."

She smiles! Her smile is clean ..

straight..

..healthy..

such is biblical marital sex
defined and lovely —

2 "Your teeth are like a flock of newly shorn ewes
Which have come up from their washing,
All of which bear twins,
And not one among them has lost her young."

3 "Your lips are like a scarlet thread,
And your mouth is lovely.
Your temples are like a slice of a pomegranate
Behind your veil."

stately, noble, righteous

4 "Your neck is like the tower of David,
Built with rows of stones
On which are hung a thousand shields,
All the round shields of the mighty men."

he approaches her gently
— touches her gently

5 "Your two breasts are like two fawns,
Twins of a gazelle
Which feed among the lilies."

all night long —

The delight of her —
breasts

6 "Until the cool of the day
When the shadows flee away,
I will go my way to the mountain of myrrh
And to the hill of frankincense."

7 "You are altogether beautiful, my darling,

And there is no blemish in you."

He Pronounces her Perfect
(c.f. Ephesians 5:27)

8 "Come with me from Lebanon, my bride;

May you come with me from Lebanon.

Journey down from the summit of Amana,

From the summit of Senir and Hermon,

From the dens of lions,

From the mountains of leopards."

Places where lions made their dens
The marital bed is a safe place

9 "You have made my heart beat faster, my sister, my bride;

You have made my heart beat faster with a single glance of your eyes,

With a single strand of your necklace."

He sees and looks upon her

10 "How beautiful is your love, my sister, my bride!

How much better is your love than wine,

And the fragrance of your oils

- Than all kinds of spices!"

He smells her

11 "Your lips, my bride, drip honey;

Honey and milk are under your tongue,

And the fragrance of your garments is like the fragrance of Lebanon."

..tastes her
..touches her..

12 "A garden locked is my sister, my bride,

A rock garden locked, a spring sealed up."

But her body has been off limits
until now..

But now her "Garden" of
her body, sexuality is his
to enjoy

13 "Your shoots are an orchard of pomegranates
With choice fruits, henna with nard plants,

14 Nard and saffron, calamus and cinnamon,
With all the trees of frankincense,
Myrrh and aloes, along with all the finest spices."

ever increasing flow of
delight

15 "You are a garden spring,
A well of fresh water,
And streams flowing from Lebanon."

The woman speaks:
Love is now "Awakened"
It is "time"

16 "Awake, O north wind,
And come, wind of the south;
Make my garden breathe out fragrance,
Let its spices be wafted abroad.
May my beloved come into his garden
And eat its choice fruits!"

her body is given to her
husband as his delight.

The man speaks:
There are "one flesh"
"MY" mentioned 9x

5:1 "I have come into my garden, my sister, my bride;
I have gathered my myrrh along with my balsam.
I have eaten my honeycomb and my honey;
I have drunk my wine and my milk.
Eat, friends;

God speaks:
They need not restrict their love.
They can enjoy each others delights

Drink and imbibe deeply, O lovers."

2 "I was asleep but my heart was awake.
A voice! My beloved was knocking:
'Open to me, my sister, my darling,
My dove, my perfect one!
For my head is drenched with dew,
My locks with the damp of the night.'

The couple resolves conflict

He comes to her bedroom....

.. after working late into the night

3 "I have taken off (my) dress,
How can I put it on again?
I have washed my feet,
How can I dirty them again?"

.. But she thinks of herself and refuses him

4 "My beloved extended his hand through the opening,
And my feelings were aroused for him."

he doesn't force upon the door. He is Gentle as a result she is aroused by Kindness

5 "I arose to open to my beloved;
And my hands dripped with myrrh,
And my fingers with liquid myrrh,
On the handles of the bolt."

he left the "calling card" of Perfume.

The very thing that kept him back.. He overcomes bad with Good..

6 "I opened to my beloved,
But my beloved had turned away and had gone!
My heart went out to him as he spoke.
I searched for him but I did not find him;
I called him but he did not answer me."

7 "The watchmen who make the rounds in the city found me,
They struck me and wounded me;
The guardsmen of the walls took away my shawl from me."

Tho the husband does not · Punish her.. She still was chastened.. Let God chasten!

His Gentleness is not Perceived as Weakness.. The woman launches into Poetry of his Kindness..
    i.e "Go find him.."
She can't live without him..
   Such is kindness..

8 "I adjure you, O daughters of Jerusalem,

If you find my beloved,

As to what you will tell him:

For I am lovesick."

i.e . what should we tell him when we find him?

9 "What kind of beloved is your beloved,

O most beautiful among women?

What kind of beloved is your beloved,

That thus you adjure us?"

from the top of his head to his feet
- She proclaims his character

shines with divine favor

Lit. "red".. like David.. It means that he is Rare...unique..

divine headship (1 Co. 11:3)

untouched by Greer.. Weakness.. (Hosea 7:9)

10 "My beloved is dazzling and ruddy,

Outstanding among ten thousand."

11 "His head is like gold, pure gold;

His locks are like clusters of dates

And black as a raven."

Gentleness
full of blessing
or "fixed".. Constant.. set.. .. unchanging..

always affectionate.. Sweet.. Kind..

12 "His eyes are like doves

Beside streams of water,

Bathed in milk,

And reposed in their setting."

13 "His cheeks are like a bed of balsam,

Banks of sweet-scented herbs;

full of Gentleness
.. and blessing..
or compliments..

His lips are lilies

Dripping with liquid myrrh."

He touches her with divine Affection

14 "His hands are rods of gold

Set with beryl;

Pure white.. Purity.. the "belly" is
the seat of the emotion..

His abdomen is carved ivory

Inlaid with sapphires."

15 "His legs are pillars of alabaster — Strong...unmoving...stedfast
Set on pedestals of pure gold; — from head to feet...Divine, beautiful
His appearance is like Lebanon — Majestic.. Lofty.. she is proud of him
Choice as the cedars."

16 "His mouth is full of sweetness. — Words evidence a heart.. His words are sweet
And he is wholly desirable.
This is my beloved and this is my friend, — all women want a man who is a best friend
O daughters of Jerusalem."

6:1 "Where has your beloved gone, Many men would put away their wives for a
O most beautiful among women? lack of Respect but she knows Right where
Where has your beloved turned, Solomon is... he has NOT left her
That we may seek him with you?"

2 "My beloved has gone down to his garden, She knows where he is
To the beds of balsam, & what he is doing
To pasture his flock in the gardens
And gather lilies."

3 "I am my beloved's and my beloved is mine, She knows who he is
He who pastures his flock among the lilies." and who she is

4 "You are as beautiful as Tirzah, my darling, She comes to him apologetic....
As lovely as Jerusalem, He is so forgiving that she doesn't
As awesome as an army with banners." have to speak

5 "Turn your eyes away from me, He is forgiving!
For they have confused me; His words are identical to the honeymoon
Your hair is like a flock of goats
That have descended from Gilead."

6 "Your teeth are like a flock of ewes
Which have come up from their washing,
All of which bear twins,
And not one among them has lost her young."

7 "Your temples are like a slice of a pomegranate
Behind your veil."

Solomon's harem
or possibilities of his harem

8 "There are sixty queens and eighty concubines,
And maidens without number;

This was the wife of his love.
She stood unique

9 But my dove, my perfect one, is unique:
She is her mother's only daughter;
She is the pure child of the one who bore her.
The maidens saw her and called her blessed,
The queens and the concubines also, and they
     praised her, saying,

His love makes her Grow
brighter and brighter
each day . .
more beautiful
More Pure . .
more Impressive

10 'Who is this that grows like the dawn,
As beautiful as the full moon,
As pure as the sun,
As awesome as an army with banners?'"

11 "I went down to the orchard of nut trees
To see the blossoms of the valley,
To see whether the vine had budded
Or the pomegranates had bloomed."

Their union.. and her body.. is continually seen as a vineyard.. a place of delight.. She wants to know if it is still delightful and fruitful... Especially after a conflict

12 "Before I was aware, my soul set me
Over the chariots of my noble people." — *Solomon exalts her to the highest status*

13 "Come back, come back, O Shulammite;
Come back, come back, that we may gaze at you!"
Why should you gaze at the Shulammite,
As at the dance of the two companies?

The daughters of Jerusalem speak..

The couple is leaving.. for a time of delight (ch. 7).. and they are dancing in delight

Making up is fun!

the female counterpart of "Solomon"

Its as if the couple is "One flesh"

The Romance continues
from her feet to the top of her head
He praises her as noble ————
Her praise is more sensuous ————
more intimate . .

wine and corn were blessings
The belly was the seat of
the emotion . . He calls her
the blessing of God

But he is still tender with her
Sexually . . Just as on their
honeymoon.

She is "expensive" . . noble
refreshing ————

Her countenance faces the
enemy to the north . . he
Praises her faithfulness . .

She is beautiful ————
. . royal . , ————
and holds Solomon slave ————
by her beauty

Her character 1-4
Her beauty 5-6 .
Her desirability 1-9

7:1 "How beautiful are your feet in sandals,
O prince's daughter!
The curves of your hips are like jewels,
The work of the hands of an artist."

2 "Your navel is like a round goblet
Which never lacks mixed wine;
Your belly is like a heap of wheat
Fenced about with lilies."

3 "Your two breasts are like two fawns,
Twins of a gazelle."

4 "Your neck is like a tower of ivory,
Your eyes like the pools in Heshbon
By the gate of Bath-rabbim;
Your nose is like the tower of Lebanon,
Which faces toward Damascus."

5 "Your head crowns you like Carmel,
And the flowing locks of your head are like purple threads;
The king is captivated by your tresses."

6 "How beautiful and how delightful you are,
My love, with all your charms!"

7 "Your stature is like a palm tree,
And your breasts are like its clusters."

8 "I said, 'I will climb the palm tree,
I will take hold of its fruit stalks.'
Oh, may your breasts be like clusters of the vine,
And the fragrance of your breath like apples,

her body is a delight

he longs for her

9 And your mouth like the best wine!"
It goes down smoothly for my beloved, ————
Flowing gently through the lips of those who fall asleep.

The woman now Responds to him
She is responsive to her husband
the couple has drunk their fill

10 "I am my beloved's, ————
And his desire is for me."

She delights in the fact that her husband longs to consume her (the meaning of "desire")

11 "Come, my beloved, let us go out into the country,
Let us spend the night in the villages."

She is also aggressive
She entices him away from the Job and off by herself.

12 "Let us rise early and go to the vineyards;
Let us see whether the vine has budded
And its blossoms have opened,
And whether the pomegranates have bloomed.
There I will give you my love."

once again the sexual intimacy is referred as a VINEYARD... a delight that nourishes...

She is creative.

13 "The mandrakes have given forth fragrance;
And over our doors are all choice fruits,
Both new and old,
Which I have saved up for you, my beloved.

mandrakes were considered as that which excited and aided in childbearing...
It is a strong "come on."

Behind doors of privacy she has delights he is accustomed to and those he has never experienced.

She is also spontaneous

One does not in Israel show open affection to a mate but one can to a brother or sister.. She is more passionate than social convention will allow

Such action was orthodox

The delight of her body ——————

a longing for her husband ——

Such love must be nurtured and awakened in time It cannot be forced or demanded

8:1 "Oh that you were like a brother to me
Who nursed at my mother's breasts.
If I found you outdoors, I would kiss you;
No one would despise me, either."

2 "I would lead you and bring you
Into the house of my mother, who used to instruct me;
I would give you spiced wine to drink from the juice of my
pomegranates."

3 "Let his left hand be under my head
And his right hand embrace me."

4 "I want you to swear, O daughters of Jerusalem,
Do not arouse or awaken my love
Until she pleases."

5 "Who is this coming up from the wilderness
Leaning on her beloved?"
Beneath the apple tree I awakened you;
There your mother was in labor with you,
There she was in labor and gave you birth."

The book ends with the couple's commitment

The apple tree was the place of love..
She was "born for" Solomon
Their love was providential

6 "Put me like a seal over your heart,
Like a seal on your arm.
For love is as strong as death,
Jealousy is as severe as Sheol;
Its flashes are flashes of fire,
The very flame of the Lord."

The Woman Speaks:
She is possessive of him

Their love is as permanent as death

..and as powerful as God's love..
Patterned on Jehovah..

7 "Many waters cannot quench love,
Nor will rivers overflow it;
If a man were to give all the riches of his house for love,
It would be utterly despised."

Their love is persevering
Nothing quenches the flame of God

and true love is precious.
It is given but not bought

8 "We have a little sister,
And she has no breasts;
What shall we do for our sister
On the day when she is spoken for?"

These verses (8-10) substantiate the divine nature of marriage.

The brothers wondered as to when their sister was able to be married.
The text is set at a time when she was a young girl..

9 "If she is a wall,
We will build on her a battlement of silver;
But if she is a door,
We will barricade her with planks of cedar."

Their reasoning: if she is moral (a wall)
we will bless her with a wedding (silver)
if immoral (a door)
we will not let her go outside
i.e. obedience to God makes one ready to marry.

10 "I was a wall, and my breasts were like towers;
Then I became in his eyes as one who finds peace."

She was obedient..
and Solomon saw her as a blessing

Here are the circumstances of their meeting.. The brothers made her work in the vineyard (1:6) She obeyed God that was difficult. Her obedience put her in the path of God's best.

11 "Solomon had a vineyard at Baal-hamon;

He entrusted the vineyard to caretakers.

Each one was to bring a thousand shekels of silver

for its fruit."

She was able to give her body (vineyard) to Solomon because her brothers cared for her fruit (8:9) Now that she was married she is thankful for their protection

12 "My very own vineyard is at my disposal;

The thousand shekels are for you, Solomon,

And two hundred are for those who take care of its fruit."

The man speaks:
She awaits his return home.
He longs to hear and listen to her voice.

13 "O you who sit in the gardens,

My companions are listening for your voice,

Let me hear it!"

The woman speaks:
She longs for him to come home to give her body to him anew

14 "Hurry, my beloved,

And be like a gazelle or a young stag

On the mountains of spices."